CHI
energy of happiness

CHI
energy of happiness

solala towler

**Andrews McMeel
Publishing**

Kansas City

Solala Towler is a musician, poet, and teacher. He is editor of *The Empty Vessel, A Journal of Contemporary Taoism*, a magazine with an international subscription and distribution base (www.abodetao.com). He is author of *A Gathering of Cranes: Bringing the Tao to the West* and *Embarking on the Way: A Guide to Western Taoism*, and in the Tao Paths series, *Love*, *Harmony, Long Life*, and *Good Fortune*. He is an instructor of Taoist meditation and of several styles of *chi kung*. He has taught classes and seminars all over the United States and abroad and is president emeritus of the **National Qigong Association** of the United States.

First published by MQ Publications Limited
12 The Ivories, 6–8 Northhampton St., London, N1 2HY

Copyright © MQ Publications Limited 2002
TEXT © Solala Towler 2002
DESIGN: Balley Design

ISBN: 0-7407-3015-0

Library of Congress Control Number on file

Printed and bound in China

CONTENTS

INTRODUCTION

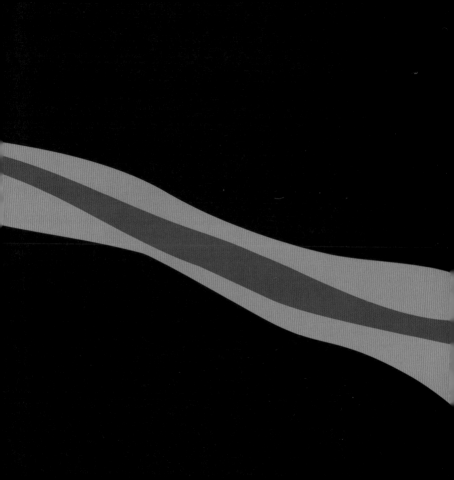

What is the true nature of happiness? For some, it is being healthy. For some, it is having a stable and fulfilling relationship. For others, it is a rewarding job or career. For yet others it is having a strong spiritual life. However, without the foundation of strong chi all these things are much more challenging and difficult to achieve.

The Chinese
say work on the
foundation of your chi first,
then all other endeavors will
unfold easily and harmoniously.

By being still, quiet, and in harmony with our emotions and our thoughts, we strengthen our chi. When we worry, when we obsess, and when we work too hard, we lose, or deplete, our chi.

By being careful where we spend our chi, we can stay strong, happy, and healthy. When we abuse ourselves by living an unhealthy lifestyle—either physically or emotionally—we waste our chi and will surely suffer for it.

Somebody with plenty of chi is fun to be around, easy to like, and exciting to work with. On the other hand, somebody with low levels of chi is often irritable, emotionally unstable, and difficult to get along with.

By taking charge of our own chi, or vital energy, we can feel more empowered, fulfilled, creative, and in control of our own lives and destinies.

In the following pages we will explore the nature of chi and how we can use it to build a strong and happy life—physically, emotionally, and spiritually.

chapter one

WHAT IS CHI?

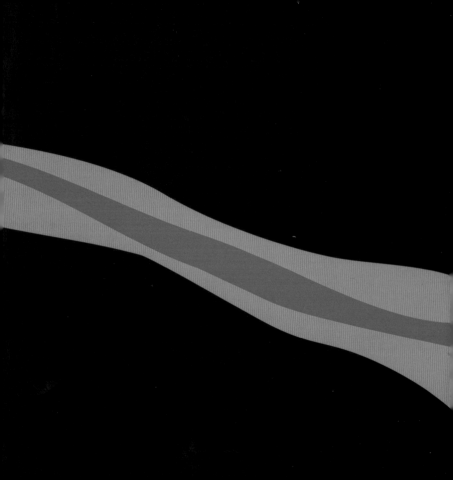

Chi (pronounced "chee") is the Chinese word for energy, life force, the animating spirit that is found in all things. The original Chinese character for "chi" shows steam rising from cooked rice. This pictorial representation shows the connection between what we eat and how we feel.

Food, however, is only one way that we acquire chi. Chi also comes from the air we breathe and from the natural world that surrounds us. This is why it is so important to eat a natural diet, free from chemical additives, and to drink lots of clean or filtered water.

There is an old saying: You are what you eat. If we subsist on a diet of low-chi foods such as prepackaged or "fast" foods, and drink too many sugar- and caffeine-filled soft drinks, our chi will be low and unstable.

If we eat lots of freshly cooked "whole foods," cooked with love and good intentions, our chi will be strong, stable, and harmonious. By adding lots of green tea, filled with natural antioxidants and anticancer properties, we can live longer, healthier, and happier lives.

Chi can be thought of as an electrical current that runs throughout our bodies, keeping our systems in good working order. It regulates our organs, directs the flow of blood and lymph in our system, and protects us from pathogens, or disease-producing agents.

Everything that lives contains chi, including plants, trees, animals, oceans, rivers, and people. Chi is what gives these things life. Where there is no chi, there is no life. At our death, chi leaves our bodies to mingle with the original source of all life, the *Tao*.

It is the amount
as well as the current or
voltage of chi in our bodies
that can have a direct and
powerful effect upon our emotions.
In Chinese medicine, each of the
five major organs (liver, heart, spleen,
lungs, and kidneys/adrenals) are
paired with a specific emotional
state, both positive
and negative.

The positive emotion connected to the liver is free-flowingness: the ability to move freely through the changes and challenges in our lives, to bend like bamboo or a new spring plant in the breeze. The negative emotion is anger, or the feeling of being bound up or "stuck" in our lives.

The positive emotions connected to the heart are joy and creativity. This is the joy of the sun-filled summer, making it a season that is connected to the heart. The negative emotion is hysteria or joy taken the extreme.

The positive emotions connected to the spleen are empathy and a sense of groundedness. Our spleen/stomach is where we feel our deep connection to the earth. The negative emotion is obsessive worry or self-absorption, and we might feel unsteady, or as though we have very shallow roots.

The positive emotion connected to the lungs is courage. Through our lungs, we breathe in chi from the atmosphere. Our lungs govern the breath used in Taoist meditation and *chi kung* (more on this later). The negative emotion is grief. It is in our chest that we feel sadness and loss.

The positive emotion connected to the kidneys and adrenals is a sense of will and determination—our "backbone." The kidneys and adrenals are the center of our sexual energy and are thought to be the repository of our prenatal chi, or *jing* (see page 29). The negative emotion is fear or anxiety; the kind of fear that wakes us in the middle of the night for no apparent reason.

Although chi is invisible to the human eye, it can be felt by everyone. We all recognize the feeling when our energy is high or low, or blocked.

When the organs and their corresponding emotional states are balanced and in harmony, we feel strong, centered, healthy, and happy. Even if one of them is weak or out of balance, our emotional life suffers. Chapter Two explores some ways to strengthen and balance these aspects of ourselves.

When flowing water comes up against a natural dam that is too high for it to surpass, it must simply stand and create a beautiful, peaceful lake. Eventually, when the water level rises above the dam, it can continue on its way.

In a similar way, when we are stopped in our tracks by some kind of obstruction in our lives, if we simply stop, pool our resources, and wait patiently until the level of chi rises again, we will be able to overcome the obstruction and continue on our way.

Sometimes, resting is the only way to replenish our chi when it is low. Taking time out to gather our chi when it has been used up by stress or hard work can be most useful. By paying closer attention to the state of our chi, we can foresee and even avoid potential problems.

Besides obtaining chi from food, water, and air, we are also born with an amount of what is called "prenatal chi" (the chi that allows unborn babies to breathe in the womb through the umbilical cord) or *jing* (often translated as "essence"). We get this from our parents at the moment of our conception.

Jing energy is said to reside in the sexual center of the kidney/adrenals. It controls our sexual energy, which like anything else can be abused or used in a healthy, even spiritual, manner. A positive attitude toward sexuality can benefit both our physical and emotional health.

At the time
of conception, our
constitutional energy is
created by our parents. Not
only our *jing* is determined, but
also our karmic destiny, or *ming*.
For this reason it is important
that during pregnancy, we
pay close attention to
our energy levels.

If the energy of our
parents was unhealthy
or uncentered at the time
of our conception,
perhaps due to emotional
problems, health
concerns, or the influence
of drugs or alcohol, it
would have a negative
effect on our *jing*.

Some people are born with a strong constitution, whereas others are born with a tendency toward illness. This may seem unfair, but oftentimes the person with the constitution of an ox will take that as freedom to abuse themselves throughout their lives, until they suddenly drop dead of a heart attack in their fifties.

The person with a weak constitution, who is prone to illness, will be forced to take better care of themselves and, in this way, live a much longer and healthier life.

The chi in our body is thought to run in specific
pathways along "meridians." These pathways
connect various organ systems to each other
in a synergistic map of our body. Along these
pathways are important points, or junctures.

Meridians can run from our feet to each organ. An acupuncturist can affect the flow of chi to the liver, for example, by inserting a needle into our big toe.

Our chi can also be enhanced or strengthened by the use of herbs or massage (called *tuina*, or *anmo*, in Chinese).

When we are filled with chi, we glow and are attractive to others. Our good chi will inspire others to be happy, too.

When we have a strong flow of chi in our
bodies, it is easier to find true happiness.
We welcome challenges and our joy
is contagious—we feel like we might
take over the world! Even our
thought processes work better
when our chi is strong.

Unhealthy habits in everyday living abuse the chi energy. Even people with strong chi must be mindful of their energy levels.

When our chi is low, blocked, or unbalanced, it is very difficult to keep our minds clear or our emotions from raging out of control.

When our chi is low,
we feel bad about
ourselves. We may
become depressed,
angry, or fearful.

If our chi is too low, it can be like trying to start a car that has run out of gas. It is important to always leave some chi in reserve, like the reserve tank of a car.

Good chi is our birthright. Pollutants, stress, trauma, and negative thinking are all emotions that block or drain our chi.

In the next chapter we'll look at ways we can build a strong chi foundation in our lives and use that foundation to attain personal fulfillment as well as long-lasting happiness.

chapter two

BUILDING A STRONG FOUNDATION

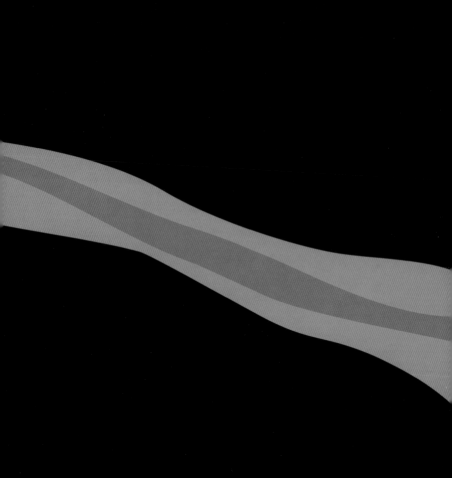

Along with eating correctly, getting the right amount of sleep and relaxation, and not wasting your chi through an unhealthy lifestyle, the best way to build a strong foundation with your chi is through the practice of *chi kung*.

Chi kung means working with chi to enhance our energy management and improve our life force. *Chi kung* is a way to access, circulate, and then store chi in our bodies.

We are surrounded by chi at all times. It is in the air that we breathe. Chi is most strongly felt when we are surrounded by nature, so it is important that we don't spend our entire lives fenced in by concrete, metal, and glass.

By connecting ourselves with the energy of the natural world around us, our chi will be strengthened and purified.

EXERCISE

Stand with your feet shoulder-width apart, arms at your sides. Concentrate on sending roots down into the earth from the soles of your feet. These roots should be at least twice the length of your body. Feel them burrow down into the earth, bringing up the good, green, healing energy into your body.

You can also practice this exercise while sitting on a chair or a meditation cushion, sending roots down into the earth from the base of your spine.

If you are in a stressful situation, you can fortify your chi by rooting yourself to the earth, using the techniques described on page 47. For example, if flying makes you anxious, concentrate on sending down roots from your feet or spine. This will keep you connected to the earth even while flying thousands of feet above it, and encourage a feeling of calm.

Take time to visit nature as often as possible. The healing powers of the natural world cannot be overemphasized. Remember that you too are a part of nature, even if you live in an urban environment. Most cities today have parks where you can sit beneath a tree, walk on the grass, or relax by a cascading fountain. Make use of them.

Sitting
on a beach and
letting the sounds of the
incoming waves wash over
you, or walking on a trail deep
in the forest, breathing in the
fresh smells of the trees, plants,
and earth, can be even more
therapeutic than a visit
to a psychotherapist
or to an expensive
health spa.

The practice of *chi kung* centers on the breath. The breath is the doorway to greater, deeper worlds of energy and spirituality.

EXERCISE

Stand comfortably with your feet shoulder-width apart. Breathe deeply. On each inhalation, imagine that you are breathing in light. Picture in your inner mind a glowing or golden energy entering your body, bringing in with it healing and peace. Allow it to fill your body. As you exhale, imagine that you are releasing all the impurities and toxins from within your body. After doing this for some time, try inhaling and exhaling light. As you inhale, light will fill your body, then, as you exhale, the light's healing properties will be released back into the world around you.

One of the secrets of chi kung practice is to slow down. You may have seen the gentle, slow movements of people doing tai chi (*taiji*) in the park. The movement in tai chi, which can look like a type of underwater ballet, is a very refreshing and energizing practice.

When we rush or are impatient, we can become easily unbalanced or upset. It is in going slowly that we can keep our balance and not lose sight of our way.

EXERCISE

Stand under a tree with your back against the trunk. Close your eyes and place your hands on your lower abdomen, fingers interlaced. Breathe slowly and deeply from your belly.

Feel your chi intermingle with that of the solid, deep-rooted tree. Empty your mind and relax, exchanging your chi with that of the tree. You will be amazed at how peaceful and refreshed you will feel after a short period.

The area of our lower abdomen, a few inches below the naval and inside our body, is of great significance in *chi kung* practice. It is called the *dan tien* or "field of elixir," and it is considered to be one of the major energy centers in the body.

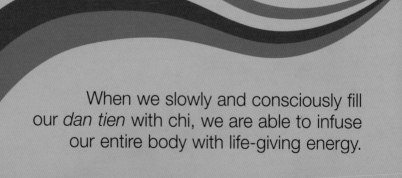

When we slowly and consciously fill our *dan tien* with chi, we are able to infuse our entire body with life-giving energy.

When practicing *chi kung*, we breathe deeply and slowly, feeling our abdomen expand with each inhalation, and contract with each exhalation. This is called natural, or prenatal breathing, which describes how unborn babies breathe in the womb through the umbilical cord.

EXERCISE

Sit quietly, either on the edge of a chair or on a cushion, with your back straight but not stiff. Place your palms down on each knee, close your eyes and breathe slowly, deeply, and gently through your nose.

Feel your *dan tien* fill with pure healing chi on each inhalation. Then, as you exhale, feel all the tensions, toxins, pain, and disease in your body flow out as a thick, black smoke.

When you have completed this exercise, rub your tummy thirty-six times in a clockwise direction with the palm of your hand, starting with big circles and making them smaller as you go along. This will enable you to store the good healing chi in your lower *dan tien*.

When we are in shock, are frightened, or in pain, we tend to breathe in short, quick gasps from our chest. When we focus on breathing in slow, deep breaths from the belly, we are able to change the internal chemistry of our body.

EXERCISE

Whenever you find yourself in a stressful or demanding situation, stop, and return to that simple breathing practice.

Breathe in, "I am strong." Breathe out, "I am at peace."

EXERCISE

You can also practice leading chi with your mind. When you are relaxed and breathing chi into your lower *dan tien*, guide it slowly to any place in your body where you have pain or disease.

You might imagine this energy as a golden light, filling your entire body, bringing relief to all the dark places where you feel pain, disease, or sadness. Feel the chi filling all these places with a soft, healing glow.

EXERCISE

An easy way to feel chi is to create a "chi ball" between your palms. Hold your hands out in front of you at shoulder or waist height, palms facing one another. Using the power of your imagination, picture a solid ball of energy between your palms, the size of a beach ball.

Slowly bring your palms together, as if you were squeezing the chi ball between them. Then expand the ball by moving your hands apart. Repeat several times, squeezing and expanding, and you should begin to feel a subtle, yet solid, rubbery presence between your palms. This is chi.

EXERCISE

Stand quietly and practice your chi breathing exercises for a few moments. Bring your arms slowly up in front of you to chest level, palms facing up. Turning your palms down, lower your hands slowly to waist level.

This exercise raises your chi to your heart center or middle dan tien, then back down to your lower *dan tien*. It is a simple and effective way to balance and center your internal energy. Try it nine times and see if you feel a difference in your sense of energy, balance, and well-being.

Chi kung is not just a healing practice, it is an approach to life itself. It is a state of mind characterized by complete relaxation and acceptance, deep meditation and love, joy and beneficence, renewal and rebirth. It is being open to the healing energy of the universe and offers healing for the whole world.

Sometimes, when our energy is low, we need to be able to relax and allow it to build back up again in its own time. Sometimes, the best thing to do is not to do anything. If we allow our chi to rise again like a stream of water building up behind a dam, it will, after time, flow naturally over the obstacles in our lives.

Chi kung practice aligns our body, mind, and spirit—*shen*—and aligns us with the universal body, mind, and spirit. By regulating our mind and emotions through breathing and gentle movement, we can facilitate a stronger and smoother form of energy throughout our bodies, giving us greater health and freedom of movement in our lives.

A greater circulation of chi in our bodies makes us more magnetic, "sexy," or attractive to others. Consequently, we will appeal to the kind of people we want in our lives.

When we base our happiness on our internal state rather than on external circumstances, we will have a better chance of maintaining that happiness into our old age.

Once we become
cocreators of our own
lives by using the
power of chi, we will
have more energy to
be of help to those
around us who
are in need.

When our chi is strong and free-flowing, we can use it in any way we choose—from creating beautiful art to applying ourselves in our work situation. We can also use it to strengthen relationships, or even to teach healing to others.

chapter three

CHI AND EMOTIONAL FULFILLMENT

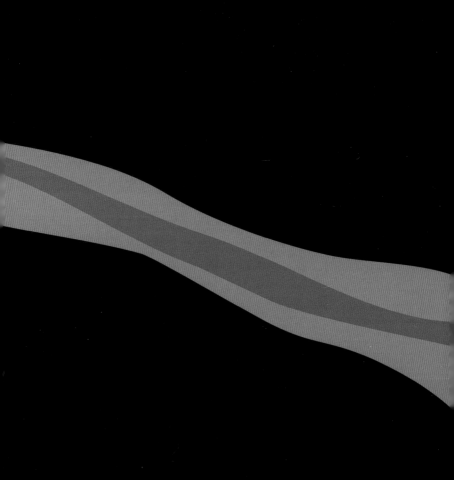

We all have our emotional ups and downs. Although some people live their lives dealing with their emotions in a balanced and harmonious way, others seem to live their lives on an emotional roller coaster, reaching great heights only to come crashing down to great depths. Anger is connected to the liver, the organ of free-flowingness. When we get frustrated, blocked, or too attached to an idea, we experience anger.

To the Chinese, emotions are simply energetic states. So, for example, the emotion of anger, a fiery, explosive type of energy, is just an energetic frequency.

Living in Western society, we are surrounded by toxins and environmental pollutants. It is easy for our livers to get overtaxed or "tight," inducing the chi state of anger. For example, alcohol heats up the liver and can induce rages.

Fear is connected to the kidney/adrenals. When we feel unsafe, exhausted, or cornered, we experience the chi state of fear or anxiety.

Just as imbalances in the organs can lead to negative emotional states, these negative emotional states can lead to problems with our organs.

In our fast-paced modern world, where everything seems to be accelerating, and where many people get through their days by drinking more and more caffeine, it is easy to burn out our adrenals and to find ourselves in a constant state of anxiety.

It is important
to note that when we
speak of the various organs,
we are speaking of them in
the Chinese sense, that is, as
energetic states. We do not
speak of them as the physical
organs themselves (although
sometimes there is a
physical aspect to
the problem).

How do we deal with our emotions as energetic states? Often it is helpful to try to gain a sense of perspective or objectivity about them. This can be difficult when we are in the middle of an intense emotional experience. At these times, all we can see or feel is what is going on right at that moment.

EXERCISE

If you find yourself in a reactive state, such as feeling anger, stop and guide the energy out of your head, where it is probably building up, down to your feet and into the earth. You can even guide it out of the end of your big toe!

EXERCISE

A good practice for gaining control of our energetic states is to stop whatever we are doing, saying, thinking, or feeling, and simply breathe. Remember to breathe from the belly, deeply and slowly.

You may want to say to yourself as you breathe in, "I am strong like a mountain." Then, as you exhale, say "I am rooted to the earth." We use these little mantras to instill within ourselves a strong sense of well-being and safety.

EXERCISE

If you wake up in the middle of the night with a panic attack, rub your palms together at least thirty-six times, making them warm. Then place them directly over your kidney in your lower back and breathe the warmth of your hands into this area at least nine times.

EXERCISE

Rub your palms over your kidneys (in your lower back) in circular motions, up from the middle and out to the sides, between nine and thirty-six times. At the same time, instill a positive feeling of safety and trust in yourself. Feel the warmth of your hands spread deeply into your body, creating feelings of safety, trust, and the ability to deal with your fears.

EXERCISE

A good practice for detoxifying the liver is to stand under a tree and point your right foot to the tree trunk. Raise your arms in front of you to shoulder height, palms facing up. Then, opening your chest by spreading your elbows, turn your palms down and bring them slowly to the level of your heart. Bring your hands slightly to the right, and guide the chi through your liver by pushing down slowly with them. Guide all the trapped, negative, or toxic chi down out of your liver, down the liver meridian on the inside of your leg, and out of your big toe into the tree, where it will be transformed into positive energy.

The area of the
stomach/spleen is where
we feel our connection to the earth
and to all living beings, or lack of it.
When our spleen center is weak, we have
problems digesting both our food and the
experiences of our lives. This can lead to
worry or self-absorption—the tendency
to go over a problem again and
again, in an endless loop.

To strengthen our spleen or earth element we need to ensure that we follow a diet that is rich in vegetables, whole grains, and organic meats, without too much intake of sugar or raw or refined foods.

Remember that emotions are simply energy states. When our chi is low or blocked, it is difficult to maintain a healthy balance of emotion. It is important not to beat ourselves up psychologically when we find ourselves in this state. Often, by working on the problem in a disciplined fashion, we can bring our emotions into balance.

For our emotions to remain harmonious they must be balanced with each other. Too much energy in one direction will often cause a reaction somewhere else.

If we can maintain our emotions in a balanced and harmonious state, we will be better able to confront the inevitable conflicts of life.

By constantly reminding ourselves that emotional states are also energetic states, we can begin to understand and even to heal some of our emotional wounds. Everyone has emotional wounds. Some of us are better able to cope with them than others. People learn to mask their wounds behind a false front. But sooner or later they will come to the surface.

Our bodies, our breath, our chi states— these are all portals into our emotional being. By accessing our emotional states we can learn to heal or at least work with them more harmoniously, and in a balanced and healthy manner.

It can be difficult to know just what our bodies need, because we cannot communicate with them directly. "Rooting" ourselves can help us feel more grounded, more solid, more present in our bodies. (See the exercise on page 47.)

The more connected we are with our bodies, the more connected we will be with our emotions. In this way we can be more objective about, and not merely the victims of, our feelings.

EXERCISE

Sit or stand quietly, breathing through your nose, deeply and slowly. Breathe in, saying "I am a mountain." Breathe out, saying "I am rooted to the earth."

Soft like a cloud,
Solid like a mountain,
I sit and await the unfolding.

—BAI YUAN

The ancient Chinese philosophers warn us that it is exactly when things are going very well for us that we should be careful. Our circumstances can change in an instant. Likewise, when things are at their worst, a seed of change is always inherent in each situation, no matter how dire.

Extremes of
any kind are not healthy.
Joy, when taken to the
extreme, will transform into
hysteria. Anger can easily turn
into depression, courage into fear.
Even the positive emotion of love,
taken to the extreme, can
transform into possessiveness
and a need to control the
person we love.

Remember that
your emotions are not
you. Emotions are energy
states which you travel
through on your life's journey.
By not identifying with any one
of them—joy or sorrow, grief or
anger, fear or anxiety—we
can explore our true
nature, which is simple,
radiant, and
eternal.

Underneath our own constantly transforming emotional states lie our true selves, our essential natures, or what the Chinese call our *Tao* natures. Changing—as a tree does in each season—yet solid and enduring, your own essential nature is simple like a seed, yet it contains the germ of eternal life.

chapter four

CHI AND
SPIRITUAL
CULTIVATION

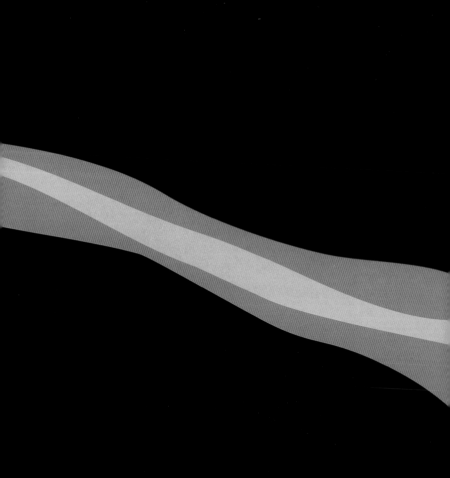

One of the basic facts of life is that we all want to be happy. We do not wish to suffer; and yet, suffering is a part of life, just as happiness is.

If we spend too much time searching for ways to avoid suffering, we will also miss out on much of the happiness that is possible in our lives.

What then to do about our suffering? Lao-tzu, the ancient Taoist author of the *Tao Te Ching*, tells us:

Accept suffering as the human condition.

Suffering comes from having a body.
Without our body, how can there be suffering?

Therefore, she who cares for her body
While serving heaven
Can be trusted
To care for the whole world.

In other words, because we are living in the material world, we cannot escape suffering. Yet if we manage to care for ourselves as well as those around us selflessly and graciously, as if we were serving heaven itself, we can then be trusted to care for the whole world.

In Taoist literature,
we come across the
term *shengjen*, which means
"authentic person." An authentic
person is someone who is able
to act completely and naturally
as their true self, no matter
what the situation.

An authentic person, sometimes called a sage, is someone who faces their suffering and their fears, as well as their joys, directly, honestly, and completely.

When the authentic person is suffering, they are engaging themselves directly and completely in their suffering, not trying to push it away, deny, or force it to end in any way.

At the same time, they are aware that the suffering experienced in that moment (or series of moments) will, sooner or later, transform into something else.

If we can enter into our suffering
as honestly and authentically as
possible, we can reduce its severity
and duration. It is often in desperate
attempts to avoid suffering at all
times and in all ways that we
create further and deeper
suffering for ourselves.

Many modern societies are built around this idea of avoiding suffering. Armed with a bewildering and dangerous arsenal of drugs we attempt to wipe out any experience of physical or emotional discomfort. However, the side effects of these drugs will often create new and even more severe suffering.

The Taoists say that life is built moment by moment—some of these moments are interesting and exciting, many of them are not. By constantly trying to achieve happiness, we often find it escaping our grasp.

By accepting suffering willingly, as a part of the human condition, we are also allowing the seed of happiness to take root in our hearts.

In the well-known *yin/yang* symbol we find the germ of light in the field of darkness, as well as the seed of darkness within the field of light. We can embrace the seed of happiness inherent in each moment of suffering.

We would also do well to recognize and embrace the seed of suffering inherent in each moment of happiness. In this way we will remain centered during moments of great happiness.

The ancient Taoists often compared the *Tao*, or spiritual reality, to water. Water is humble; it always seeks the lowest level. Water conforms to whatever shape it finds itself in. Though soft, water will in time carve through solid rock. In the same way, if we are humble, adaptable, and patient, we can cut through the obstacles in our lives and discover the flow of Tao.

If we build our happiness on simple things like love, friendship, good health, and spirit, we can build a sense of happiness that will endure the challenges and changes that life gives us.

When we depend on material things—luxury, fame, or fortune—for our happiness, then it becomes a fragile thing, easily destroyed or lost.

The Chinese have a term, *wu wei*, which means "not doing," or rather "not doing anything outside the natural flow." To live our lives according to the principle of *wu wei*, we must learn to slow down and become sensitive to the currents of change in each moment. Thereby, we will always know the correct thing to do or not to do.

Wu wei means being able to understand how each action defines or shapes the one coming after it. With this knowledge, we can then best judge what the correct response to any given situation should be.

If we are being true to our essential nature,
we can always respond in an authentic,
spontaneous, and direct manner.

Wu wei can also be taken to mean "don't push the river." Often any one decision we make will have various ramifications further down the line. If we pay attention to our actions at the beginning, we can often save ourselves from problems at the end.

In dwelling, live close to the earth.
In your meditation, become a deep pool.
With others, be gentle and benevolent.
In speech, be trustworthy and sincere.
In governing, be fair and righteous.
In dealing with others, be just and fair.
In action, watch the timing.

—LAO-TZU

Wu wei can also mean "not taking credit for one's actions." When we do things in a selfless fashion, unattached to a particular outcome, we free ourselves from self-blame or disappointment.

By paying attention to the details of timing, we can know better how to act in any situation. Thus we can know what to do or "not do" at any time. This knowledge can lead to success, accomplishment, and a sense of happiness that comes from doing each thing in its right time and in the right way.

When we are born our bodies are soft and weak.
When we die our bodies are hard and stiff.
Tender plants are soft and fragile.
At their death they are dry and brittle.
Therefore the stiff and unbending are followers of death.
The flexible and yielding are followers of life.

—LAO-TZU

If we are flexible, if we can bend like the bamboo or the spring grasses, we will be better able to flow with the challenges of life and profit from our losses.

It is fine to want success and prosperity in our lives so long as we do not sacrifice our spiritual self to get them. In the end, our spiritual selves are all that we truly have.

Wu wei means not doing anything that is against our true nature. When we pretend or attempt to be someone we are not in order to impress or fool other people, nine times out of ten it will backfire on us. But if we just present ourselves naturally, warts and all, we can have an authentic experience and lead a richer, more satisfying life.

By going slowly, watching the timing, and remembering that all life is change, that each unfolding moment is a gift and an opportunity for transformation, we can live a life of richness, completeness, and happiness.

By allowing ourselves to be stiff and unyielding in mind and body, we become like dead and brittle plants. By remaining flexible, both in mind and body, we can retain that childlike sense of wonder and excitement about life. Just remember that being childlike is different from being childish.

We can be as flexible and yielding as the tender new plant while still sinking our roots deeply into the earth.